THE COOK'S COLLECTION

SUPER
SALADS

Author: Annette Wolter
Photography: Odette Teubner,
Translated by UPS Translations, London
Edited by Josephine Bacon

CLB 4154
This edition published in 1995 by Grange Books
an imprint of Grange Books PLC, The Grange, Grange Yard, London SE1 3AG
This material published originally under the series title "Kochen Wie Noch Nie"
by Gräfe und Unzer Verlag GmbH, München
© 1995 Gräfe und Unzer Verlag GmbH, München
English translation copyright: © 1995 by CLB Publishing, Godalming, Surrey
Typeset by Image Setting, Brighton, E. Sussex
Printed and bound in Singapore
All rights reserved
ISBN 1-85627-780-1

THE COOK'S COLLECTION
✽
SUPER SALADS

Annette Wolter

Introduction

With today's emphasis on healthy eating, the salad has become a popular everyday dish and not something reserved just for the summer months. Raw eating is deemed healthy eating, with salad vegetables being packed full of vitamins and minerals. Conversely, they are not packed full of calories, so as long as the dressing and accompanying ingredients are not too rich, salads also have wide appeal among calorie-conscious diners. Today's diet gurus tell us we should, ideally, eat a mixed salad every day.

Many cooks only have a handful of standard salads in their repertoire which, if eaten on a daily basis, can become repetitive. In the past a salad was traditionally a bowl of lettuce, cucumber and tomato. This, if the ingredients are freshly bought and prepared, and if an interesting dressing is served as an accompaniment, can be invigorating and refreshing. However, it is no wonder that many people consider them to be dull if this is their total experience of salads. Today, there is certainly no lack of variety of fresh salad leaves. Chinese leaves, spinach, radicchio, lamb's lettuce and endive all offer tasty alternatives to the round or Iceberg lettuce, and they are readily obtainable from most supermarkets.

The opportunity to be creative with salads has never been greater. The ingredients are waiting to be bought, and the ideas in this book will guide you through a whole spectrum of delightfully tempting ideas ranging from the light and delicate to the hearty and substantial. These recipes make use of everything from fruit and pasta to tofu and beans, and give you a base from which to branch out and experiment with any fresh ingredients you have to hand. This colourful collection will inspire every cook to mix tastes and textures in a healthy and delicious new way.

Each recipe serves four, unless otherwise indicated

Mussel Cocktail

2 garlic cloves
1 kg/2¼lbs mussels
125ml/4fl oz dry white wine
Juice of 1 lemon
6 tbsps olive oil
Salt and freshly ground white pepper
2 tbsps snipped chives
½ tsp finely chopped fresh marjoram
350g/11oz button mushrooms
1 large lemon

Preparation time:
1 hour
Standing time:
30 minutes
Nutritional value:
Analysis per serving, approx:
- 670kJ/160kcal
- 14g protein
- 6g fat
- 7g carbohydrate

Finely chop the garlic. • Scrub the mussels under running water and pull away the beard. Discard any that do not close immediately when sharply tapped. • Bring the wine to the boil, add the mussels and garlic, cover and cook over a high heat for about 10 minutes, shaking the pan from time to time. Drain and discard any mussels that have not opened. Leave to cool, then remove the shells. • Beat together the lemon juice and olive oil, and season to taste with salt and pepper. Add the chives and marjoram. • Trim, wash and thinly slice the mushrooms. Place in a bowl with the mussels. Pour over the dressing and mix carefully. • Leave to stand for 30 minutes. • Thinly slice the lemon and line a bowl with the lemon slices. Arrange the mussel salad on top.

Breast of Goose with Peppers

1 red pepper
1 green pepper
1 yellow pepper
1 red chilli
2 shallots
1 garlic clove
100g/4oz mushrooms
25g/1oz butter
Salt and freshly ground black pepper
2 tbsps lemon juice
Pinch of sugar
3 tbsps sesame oil
1 tbsp finely chopped fresh lemon balm
150g/5½oz smoked goose breast, thinly sliced

Preparation time:
25 minutes
Nutritional value:
Analysis per serving, approx:
- 500kJ/120kcal
- 11g protein
- 6g fat
- 6g carbohydrate

Wash and seed the peppers, and slice into thin rings. • Halve, seed and wash the chilli, and slice into very thin strips. • Peel and finely chop the shallots and garlic. • Wash, trim, and finely chop the mushrooms. • Melt the butter in a pan and fry the shallots and garlic until translucent. Add the mushrooms and fry, stirring frequently, until the liquid has been absorbed. Season to taste with salt and pepper and leave to cool. • Beat together the lemon juice, sugar and oil, and season to taste with salt and pepper. Stir in the mushroom mixture and the lemon balm. • Arrange the pepper rings decoratively on four plates, sprinkle over the chilli strips and top with the mushroom mixture. Place the slices of goose breast at the side.

Lamb's Lettuce Salad with Pork Fillet

250g/8oz lamb's lettuce
50g/2oz rindless smoked streaky bacon
300g/10oz pork fillet
1 tsp vegetable oil
Salt and freshly ground black pepper
2 tbsps white wine vinegar
1 tsp medium-hot mustard
6 tbsps walnut oil

Preparation time:
30 minutes
Nutritional value:
Analysis per serving, approx:
- 1090kJ/260kcal
- 16g protein
- 21g fat
- 2g carbohydrate

Discard any tough outer leaves from the lettuce. Wash thoroughly and shake dry. • Dice the bacon finely. • Heat the vegetable oil in a pan, and fry the bacon over a moderate heat until crisp. Drain on absorbent paper. • Fry the pork fillet in the bacon fat for about 10 minutes. Season to taste with salt and pepper. Wrap the pork in aluminium foil and leave to stand. • Beat together the vinegar and mustard and walnut oil, and season to taste with salt and pepper. • Add the lamb's lettuce to the dressing and divide it between four plates. • Slice the pork and arrange several slices on each plate beside the salad. Drizzle a little dressing onto the meat, then scatter over the bacon.

Artichoke Cocktail

15g/½oz clarified butter
250g/8oz boneless chicken breasts, skinned
2 egg yolks
Salt
1 tbsp lemon juice
125ml/4fl oz vegetable oil
1 garlic clove
6 tbsps tomato ketchup
1 tbsp clear honey
Pinch of cayenne pepper
8 canned artichoke hearts
150g/5½oz cooked ham
1 punnet cress
16 pimiento-stuffed olives

Preparation time:
30 minutes
Nutritional value:
Analysis per serving, approx:
- 2010kJ/480kcal
- 31g protein
- 36g fat
- 9g carbohydrate

Melt the clarified butter in a pan. Fry the chicken over a moderate heat for 4 minutes on each side. Remove from the pan and leave to cool. • Beat together the egg yolks, salt and lemon juice. Add the oil drop by drop at first, then in a slow, steady stream, beating all the time. • Crush the garlic into the mayonnaise, and add the ketchup, honey, cayenne pepper and 2-3 tbsps water. • Drain the artichoke hearts and cut into quarters. • Dice the ham and slice the chicken. • Rinse the cress and shake dry. • Divide half the mayonnaise between four plates. Arrange the artichoke hearts, chicken, olives, ham and cress on top. Pour over the remaining mayonnaise.

Fruit on Iceberg Lettuce Salad

1 small iceberg lettuce
1 tbsp tarragon or white wine vinegar
Salt and freshly ground white pepper
2 tbsps sunflower oil
3 celery sticks
250g/8oz strawberries
1 honeydew melon
1 avocado pear
200g/7oz cooked peeled prawns
2 tbsps lemon juice
125ml/4fl oz double cream
3 tbsps mayonnaise
1 tbsp brandy
Pinch of sugar
1 lemon balm sprig (optional)

Preparation time:
30 minutes
Nutritional value:
Analysis per serving, approx:
- 1800kJ/430kcal • 14g protein
- 34g fat
- 18g carbohydrate

Separate the lettuce leaves, rinse under cold water and drain. Beat together the vinegar, salt to taste and the oil. Line a bowl with the lettuce leaves and drizzle over the dressing. • Remove any stringy parts from the celery sticks, wash, pat dry and slice finely. • Rinse, hull and halve the strawberries. Cut any large ones into quarters. • Halve the melon and remove the seeds. Scoop out the flesh using a melon baller. • Halve, stone and peel the avocado pear. Dice the flesh. • Mix the prawns with the fruit, and sprinkle over the lemon juice. • Whip the cream until fairly stiff, then add the mayonnaise, pepper, brandy and sugar. • Pile the fruit salad onto the lettuce leaves and chill. • Spoon the creamy dressing onto the salad. Sprinkle over the lemon balm leaves, if using.

Chinese Leaf and Orange Salad

1 small head Chinese leaves
1 orange
50g/2oz walnut halves
50g/2oz raisins
75ml/3fl oz single cream
1 tbsp walnut oil
Juice of ½ lemon
1 tbsp apple juice
100g/4oz cottage cheese
½ tsp chopped fresh or ¼ tsp dried rosemary

Preparation time:
15 minutes
Nutritional value:
Analysis per serving, approx:
- 1100kJ/260kcal
- 7g protein
- 17g fat
- 18g carbohydrate

Wash and drain the Chinese leaves and cut into very thin strips. • Peel the orange, remove the pith and pips and separate into segments. Reserve 4 segments for the garnish and chop the remainder. • Reserve 4 walnut halves and coarsely chop the remainder. Place the Chinese leaves, chopped orange, chopped nuts and the raisins in a salad bowl. • Beat together the cream, oil, lemon juice and apple juice. Pour over the salad and toss lightly. Carefully stir in the cottage cheese and rosemary. Garnish the salad with the reserved orange segments and walnut halves.

Coconut Fruit Platter

1 carrot
50g/2oz raisins
Juice of ½ lime
100g/4oz fresh coconut (about ⅓ of a coconut)
8 fresh dates
1 mango
1 avocado pear
125ml/4fl oz double cream
2 tsps clear honey
Freshly ground white pepper
Lemon balm sprig

Preparation time:
20 minutes
Nutritional value:
Analysis per serving, approx:
- 1900kJ/450kcal
- 4g protein
- 29g fat
- 42g carbohydrate

Peel and coarsely grate the carrot. Place in a bowl, add the raisins and 2 tsps lime juice and mix thoroughly. • Thinly slice the coconut. • Wash, drain, halve and stone the dates. • Peel and stone the mango, and dice the flesh. • Peel, halve and stone the avocado pear, and thinly slice the flesh. • Arrange the prepared ingredients decoratively on four plates. Drizzle 2 tsps lime juice onto the avocado pear slices to prevent discolouration. • Whip the cream until fairly stiff, then add the honey, the remaining lime juice and a little pepper. • Spoon the creamy dressing onto the centre of each plate and, if liked, season with freshly ground pepper. Garnish with lemon balm leaves.

Cucumber and Prawn Salad

1 cucumber
Salt
2 tbsps white wine vinegar
1 tbsp soya sauce
½ tsp sugar
3 tbsps sunflower oil
200g/7oz cooked peeled prawns
3 tbsps chopped fresh dill
2 hard-boiled eggs, shelled

Preparation time:
30 minutes
Nutritional value:
Analysis per serving, approx:
- 710kJ/170kcal
- 15g protein
- 11g fat
- 2g carbohydrate

Wash the cucumber in tepid water, dry and cut in half lengthways. Remove the seeds with a spoon, and chop the flesh into ½cm/¼-inch cubes. • Combine ½ tsp salt, the vinegar, soya sauce and sugar, stirring until the sugar and salt have completely dissolved. Beat in the sunflower oil, and add the prawns and cucumber cubes. • Arrange the salad in a bowl and sprinkle over the dill. • Chop the eggs lengthways into eight and place on top of the salad. • Freshly baked wholemeal rolls are a tasty accompaniment.

Oakleaf Lettuce with Smoked Salmon

1 small head of oakleaf lettuce
300g/10oz button mushrooms
2 tbsps lemon juice
2 shallots
2-3 tbsps balsamic or white wine vinegar
Salt and freshly ground black pepper
½ tsp dried tarragon
4 tbsps olive oil
200g/7oz smoked salmon
1 tbsp chopped fresh parsley

Preparation time:
45 minutes
Nutritional value:
Analysis per serving, approx:
- 670kJ/160kcal
- 14g protein
- 9g fat
- 6g carbohydrate

Wash and dry the lettuce leaves. Cut any large leaves in half or into quarters. • Trim, wash and finely slice the mushrooms. Toss in the lemon juice to prevent discolouration. • Peel and finely chop the shallots. • Beat together the vinegar, salt and pepper to taste, tarragon, shallots and olive oil. • Toss the salad leaves and mushroom slices in the dressing and arrange them on four plates. • Cut the smoked salmon into eight equal-sized slices, and arrange two slices on each plate. Sprinkle over the parsley and serve the salad with fresh French bread and butter.

Cucumber Cocktail

2 small heads of chicory
1 small cucumber
1 seedless orange
2 ripe pears
2 tbsps freshly squeezed lime juice
Sea salt and freshly ground black pepper
125ml/4fl oz double cream
1 tbsp walnut oil
1 tbsp maple syrup
$^1/_2$ tsp Dijon mustard
50g/2oz walnut halves
150g/5$^1/_2$oz cooked peeled prawns
1 tbsp finely chopped fresh dill
4 dill sprigs

Preparation time:
20 minutes
Nutritional value:
Analysis per serving, approx:
- 1800kJ/430kcal
- 12g protein
- 31g fat
- 21g carbohydrate

Trim the chicory and remove the centres of the stems. Separate the chicory into leaves, wash and leave to drain. • Peel and dice the cucumber. • Peel the orange, remove the pith and divide into segments. Chop coarsely. • Wash, dry, quarter and core the pears. Chop coarsely. • Season the lime juice with sea salt and pepper to taste. Stir in the cream, walnut oil, maple syrup and mustard, mixing thoroughly. • Place the cucumber, orange, pears, walnuts, prawns and chopped dill in a bowl, pour over the dressing and toss lightly. Arrange the chicory leaves decoratively around the edges of 4 sundae glasses, spoon the salad into the centre and garnish with the dill sprigs.

Fennel and Turkey Salad

250ml/9fl oz crème fraîche
1 egg yolk
1 tbsp finely grated fresh Parmesan cheese
2 tbsps lemon juice
Salt and freshly ground white pepper
Pinch of sugar
Pinch of cinnamon
1 orange
1 apple
2 spring onions
200g/7oz cooked sliced turkey breast
2 fennel bulbs
100g/4oz stoned fresh dates

Preparation time:
30 minutes
Standing time:
15 minutes
Nutritional value:
Analysis per serving, approx:
- 2100kJ/500kcal
- 21g protein
- 34g fat
- 28g carbohydrate

Combine the crème fraîche, egg yolk, cheese and lemon juice. Season to taste with salt and pepper, and stir in the sugar and cinnamon. • Peel the orange and remove the pith. Divide into segments, cutting the skin away from each segment, and retaining as much of the juice as possible. Add the orange segments and juice to the dressing. • Wash, quarter and core the apple. Dice the quarters, and stir immediately into the dressing. • Trim the spring onions and thinly slice the white and pale green parts. • Cut the turkey breast into strips. • Reserve the tender green feathery leaves of the fennel for the garnish. Wash the bulbs, and cut into thin strips. • Cut the dates in half. • Stir the fennel, onions, dates and turkey into the dressing. • Leave to stand for 15 minutes, then serve garnished with the fennel leaves.

Tuna Fish Salad

250g/8oz onions
Salt and freshly ground white pepper
2 round lettuces
1½ tbsps red wine vinegar
6 tbsps olive oil
1 tsp Dijon mustard
1 tbsp finely chopped fresh tarragon
4 tbsps finely chopped fresh parsley
300g/10oz canned tuna fish, drained
4 hard-boiled eggs, shelled

Preparation time:
20 minutes
Nutritional value:
Analysis per serving, approx:
- 1800kJ/430kcal
- 32g protein
- 27g fat
- 10g carbohydrate

Thinly slice the onions and push out into rings. Place in a salad bowl and sprinkle with salt. • Trim and wash the lettuces, shake dry and tear into smaller pieces. • Beat together the vinegar, oil and mustard, and season to taste with pepper. Add half the tarragon and half the parsley to the dressing. • Flake the fish, and cut the eggs into eight. Add the fish and eggs to the onion rings, and pour over the dressing. Add the lettuce and remaining herbs. • Toss gently just before serving. • Serve with fresh French bread.

Greek Salad

2 beefsteak tomatoes
1 small cucumber
1 green pepper
200g/7oz Feta cheese
1 red skin onion
1 garlic clove
3 tbsps red wine vinegar
¼ tsp dry mustard
½ tsp dried oregano
3 tbsps extra-virgin olive oil
Salt and freshly ground black pepper
50g/2oz black olives

Preparation time:
20 minutes
Nutritional value:
Analysis per serving, approx:
- 920kJ/220kcal
- 9g protein
- 15g fat
- 12g carbohydrate

Wash and dry the tomatoes, and cut into eight. • Wash and dry the cucumber. Slice thickly. • Halve, seed, wash and dry the pepper. Cut into strips. • Crumble the Feta cheese. • Peel and thinly slice the onion and push out into rings. • Place the onion, cheese, pepper, cucumber and tomatoes in a bowl and mix gently. • Crush the garlic and mix together with the vinegar, mustard and oregano. Gradually beat in the olive oil. Season to taste with salt and pepper. • Drizzle the dressing over the salad. Add the olives. • Freshly baked garlic bread and a Greek red wine round off this salad beautifully.

Pepper and Salami Salad

2 green peppers
1 red pepper
1 yellow pepper
1 large Spanish onion
100g/4oz thinly-sliced salami
2 tbsps finely chopped fresh parsley
2 garlic cloves
Salt and freshly ground black pepper
3 tbsps red wine vinegar
2 tbsps sunflower oil

Preparation time:
20 minutes
Standing time:
8-10 minutes
Nutritional value:
Analysis per serving, approx:
- 880kJ/210kcal
- 7g protein
- 17g fat
- 9g carbohydrate

Halve, seed and wash the peppers, and cut into thin strips. • Peel and thinly slice the onions and push out into rings. • Cut the salami slices into quarters and combine them with the peppers and onion rings in a salad bowl. • Sprinkle over the parsley. • Crush the garlic cloves with the salt, and stir in the vinegar, oil and pepper. Pour the dressing onto the salad, toss, and leave to stand for 8-10 minutes. • Buttered, toasted wholemeal bread or freshly-baked farmhouse bread are delicious accompaniments.

Our Tip: To add a spicy touch, seed a small, hot chilli, cut into thin strips and toss with the salad.

Radicchio and Cheese Salad

1 large radicchio
200g/7oz mushrooms
2 red skin onions
150g/5¹/₂oz Emmental cheese
1 dessert pear
1 tsp French mustard
2 tbsps tarragon vinegar
Salt and freshly ground black pepper
2 tbsps walnut oil
2 tbsps snipped chives

Preparation time:
30 minutes
Nutritional value:
Analysis per serving, approx:
- 1090kJ/260kcal
- 14g protein
- 16g fat
- 15g carbohydrate

Separate the radicchio leaves, wash and shake dry. Tear into pieces. • Trim and wash the mushrooms, pat dry and slice thinly. • Peel and thinly slice the onions and push out into rings. Cut the cheese into thin strips. • Peel, core and quarter the pear. Thinly slice the quarters. • Combine the mustard, vinegar, salt and pepper. Beat in the oil. Put the salad ingredients in a bowl, pour over the dressing and toss well. • Garnish with the snipped chives. • This salad is particularly delicious served with crusty French bread.

Courgette Salad with Black Olives

600g/1½lbs small courgettes
Ice cubes
1 beefsteak tomato
1 white onion
3 tbsps lemon juice
5 tbsps olive oil
Salt and freshly ground white pepper
3 mint sprigs
5-6 individual rosemary leaves
12 stoned black olives
50g/2oz Mozzarella cheese

Chilling time:
3 hours
Preparation time:
25 minutes
Nutritional value:
Analysis per serving, approx:
- 760kJ/180kcal
- 7g protein
- 10g fat
- 15g carbohydrate

Wash and trim the courgettes. Place them in a bowl with a little water and some ice cubes, and chill in the refrigerator for about 3 hours. • Wash and dry the tomato. Cut into eight. • Peel the onion and cut into thin strips. • Beat together the lemon juice and olive oil, and season to taste with salt and pepper. • Wash the mint and pinch off the leaves, reserving some for the garnish. Finely chop the remainder. Chop the rosemary leaves and stir into the dressing with the chopped mint. • Drain and dice the courgettes. Place the courgettes, tomato, onion and black olives in a bowl, pour over the dressing and toss lightly. • Dice the cheese and scatter it over the top. Garnish with the reserved mint leaves.

Celery and Endive Salad

500g/1lb 2oz celery
½ head of endive
3 tbsps wine vinegar
4 tbsps olive oil
1 tsp American mustard
Salt and freshly ground black pepper
2 tbsps mayonnaise
100g/4oz cooked ham
1 tart apple
100g/4oz mushrooms preserved in oil

Preparation time:
30 minutes
Nutritional value:
Analysis per serving, approx:
- 880kJ/210kcal
- 8g protein
- 12g fat
- 17g carbohydrate

Trim the celery head, and separate into sticks. Remove the leaves, wash them and cut into fine strips. Wash and drain the sticks, and cut into ½cm/¼-inch pieces. • Discard the green outer leaves of the endive and separate the yellow leaves. Wash under warm running water. Shake dry and chop into very thin strips. • Beat together the vinegar, olive oil and mustard, and season to taste with salt and pepper. Stir in the mayonnaise. • Dice the ham. Peel, quarter, core and dice the apple. • Drain the mushrooms and place in a bowl with the celery, endive, ham and apple. Pour over the dressing and toss well. Sprinkle over the celery leaves. • Serve well-chilled.

Sicilian Shallots

750g/1lb 11oz shallots
Salt and freshly ground white pepper
6 tbsps olive oil
1 tsp sugar
125ml/4fl oz white wine vinegar

Preparation time:
40 minutes
Nutritional value:
Analysis per serving, approx:
- 460kJ/110kcal
- 3g protein
- 4g fat
- 16g carbohydrate

Peel the shallots. Place in a pan, cover with lightly salted water and cook for about 10 minutes until just tender but still firm. Drain. • Heat the oil in a large frying pan, add the shallots in a single layer and gently fry on all sides. Sprinkle over the sugar and fry for a further 4-5 minutes, turning gently. Add the vinegar and season with salt and pepper. • Leave to cool and serve as an hors d'oeuvre with cold meat or smoked fish.

Our Tip: *This marinated vegetable dish, which may be served as a starter or side dish, stores well. After adding the vinegar, transfer the shallots, while still hot, to a clean screw-top jar and seal immediately. When cold, store in the refrigerator. They will keep for several days.* • *If shallots are not available, use onions, chopping up any larger ones.* • *This salad tastes delicious with the addition of a green and a red pepper. Seed and wash the peppers, cut into thin strips and blanch in lightly salted water for 2-3 minutes. Drain and fry with the shallots or onion.*

Tomato Salad

500g/1lb 2oz small, ripe tomatoes
3 shallots
Salt and freshly ground black pepper
1 tbsp white wine vinegar
1 tsp lemon juice
3 tbsps olive oil
½ bunch of thyme

Preparation time:
20 minutes
Nutritional value:
Analysis per serving, approx:
- 280kJ/67kcal
- 2g protein
- 4g fat
- 6g carbohydrate

Wash and dry the tomatoes. Slice and arrange decoratively on a salad dish. • Peel and finely chop the shallots. Scatter them over the tomatoes. • Season the salad evenly with salt and pepper to taste. • Mix together the wine vinegar, lemon juice and olive oil, and pour over the salad. • Rinse the thyme in warm water, shake dry, discard any tough stalks and chop finely. Scatter the thyme over the salad before serving. • Depending on the accompanying main course, you may like to serve this salad with triangles of thinly-sliced, wholemeal bread.

Our Tip: If you prefer to use large beefsteak tomatoes, wash and dry them, then chop into 3cm/1-inch cubes. Retain any juice and seeds, and add these to the salad dressing, as they contain valuable nutrients.

Four Seasons Salad

2 tomatoes
Salt and freshly ground white pepper
1 small shallot
½ cucumber
1 large bunch of radishes
1 small lettuce or endive
1 punnet cress
1-2 tbsps cider vinegar
Pinch of sugar
3 tbsps sunflower oil
1 slice white bread

Preparation time:
30 minutes
Nutritional value:
Analysis per serving, approx:
- 670kJ/160kcal
- 6g protein
- 6g fat
- 21g carbohydrate

Wash and dry the tomatoes, and cut into eight wedges. Arrange the wedges on one quarter of a large salad dish, and sprinkle with salt. • Peel and finely chop the shallot, and scatter over the tomatoes. • Wash the cucumber, and cut into ½ cm/½-inch thick sticks. • Trim, wash and dry the radishes. Cut them into slices. • Discard the outer leaves of the lettuce or endive. Separate the remaining leaves, wash and shake dry. Slice coarsely. • Arrange each vegetable on a separate part of the salad dish. • Cut the cress, rinse and drain. • Stir the sugar into the vinegar, and season with salt and pepper to taste. Stir in 2 tbsps sunflower oil, and pour the salad dressing over the salad. • Dice the bread. Heat the remaining oil in a pan, and fry the bread cubes until crisp. • Garnish the salad with the cress and croûtons.

Golden Salad

2 heads of chicory
2 yellow peppers
300g/10oz canned sweetcorn
2 celery sticks
4 tbsps low-fat curd cheese
1 tsp clear honey
1-2 tbsps cider vinegar
1 tbsp sunflower oil
Pinch of sugar
Salt and freshly ground white pepper
4 tbsps sprouting wheat grains

Preparation time:
35 minutes
Nutritional value:
Analysis per serving, approx:
• 880kJ/210kcal
• 9g protein
• 5g fat
• 33g carbohydrate

Trim the chicory, cut out the centres of the stems and wash the leaves. • Halve, seed and wash the peppers. Dry and cut into strips. • Drain the sweetcorn. • Trim and wash the celery and pull off any tough strings. Cut the sticks into $^1/_2$ cm/$^1/_4$-inch thick slices. • Arrange the chicory, peppers, sweetcorn and celery next to one another on a salad platter. Alternatively, mix together in a large salad bowl. • Mix together the curd cheese, honey, cider vinegar, oil and sugar, and season to taste with salt and pepper to give a sweet-and-sour dressing. Pour the dressing over the salad and toss lightly. Rinse the sprouting wheat grains, drain well and scatter over the salad.

Mixed Salad

To serve 6:
1 garlic clove
1 head of endive or lollo rosso
1 bunch of spring onions
400g/14oz tomatoes
2 small courgettes
1 bunch of radishes
1 red skin onion
1 yellow pepper
2 celery sticks
3 tbsps olive oil
Pinch of sugar
3 tbsps herb vinegar
Salt and freshly ground black pepper
3 tbsps finely chopped fresh mixed herbs (such as basil, chives and Tarragon)

Preparation time:
30 minutes
Nutritional value:
Analysis per serving, approx:
- 750kJ/180kcal
- 8g protein
- 5g fat
- 25g carbohydrate

Cut the garlic clove in half and rub the inside of a salad bowl with the cut edges. • Trim and cut the endive or lollo rosso into thick strips, rinse under cold water and drain well. • Trim and wash the spring onions, and cut into rings. • Wash and dry the tomatoes and cut into eight. • Trim and wash the courgettes and the radishes. Dry and slice. • Peel and thinly slice the onion and push out into rings. • Halve, seed and wash the pepper. Cut into strips. • Trim, wash and slice the celery. • Beat the oil and sugar into the vinegar, and season to taste with salt and pepper. • Mix the prepared salad ingredients with the dressing and garnish with the chopped herbs.

Lamb's Lettuce with Radicchio

100g/4oz lamb's lettuce
1 radicchio
3 clementines
1 small white onion
1 small apple
3 tbsps cider vinegar
1 tsp maple syrup
2 tbsps walnut oil
Salt and freshly ground white pepper

Preparation time:
20 minutes
Standing time:
10 minutes
Nutritional value:
Analysis per serving, approx:
- 1090kJ/260kcal
- 12g protein
- 21g fat
- 8g carbohydrate

Trim, wash and drain the lamb's lettuce. • Separate the radicchio into leaves, wash and leave to drain. • Peel the clementines, separate into segments, remove the membrane and cut the segments in half. • Peel and finely chop the onion. Shred the radicchio. Place the lamb's lettuce, radicchio, clementines and onion in a salad bowl and mix carefully. • Peel, core and grate the apple. Mix together the apple, vinegar, syrup, and oil, and season to taste with salt and pepper. Add the apple dressing to the salad.

Our Tip: *The clementine segments can be replaced by 200g/7oz finely sliced mushrooms. Make the dressing with lemon juice, sunflower oil and salt and pepper.*

Radicchio with Roquefort Dressing

1 large radicchio
$^1/_2$ punnet cress
100g/4oz shelled walnuts
100g/4oz Roquefort cheese
1 tbsp red wine vinegar
150ml/5fl oz natural yogurt
Salt and freshly ground black pepper

Preparation time:
25 minutes
Nutritional value:
Analysis per serving, approx:
• 500kJ/120kcal
• 2g protein
• 5g fat
• 16g carbohydrate

Separate the radicchio leaves, wash, and leave to drain. • Wash the cress, pat dry, and chop finely. • Coarsely chop the walnuts. • Mash the Roquefort cheese with a fork and mix with the vinegar and yogurt. Season to taste with salt and pepper. • Shred the radicchio and combine with the cress and nuts in a salad bowl. Pour over the Roquefort dressing, cover and leave to stand for 10 minutes before serving.

Our Tip: Other blue cheeses, such as Gorgonzola or Cambazola, may also be used instead of Roquefort in the dressing.

Herring and Cucumber Salad

4 tbsps double cream
4 tbsps natural yogurt
1 tbsp lemon juice
$^{1}/_{2}$ small onion
1 bunch dill
1 bunch parsley
1 bunch chives
Pinch of sugar
Salt and freshly ground black pepper
$^{1}/_{2}$ cucumber
1 bunch radishes
4-8 lettuce leaves
4 rollmops or soused herring fillets
$^{1}/_{2}$ lemon, cut into wedges

Preparation time:
20 minutes
Nutritional value:
Analysis per serving, approx:
- 1390kJ/330kcal
- 18g protein
- 27g fat
- 7g carbohydrate

Whip the cream until stiff and combine with the yogurt and lemon juice. • Peel and finely grate the onion, and stir into the yogurt and cream mixture. • Wash the dill, parsley and chives and shake dry. Reserve a few dill and parsley sprigs for the garnish, and finely chop the remainder. Snip the chives. Stir the herbs and sugar into the dressing, and season to taste with salt and pepper. • Peel the cucumber, cut in half lengthways and remove the seeds with a spoon. Thinly slice the cucumber. • Trim and wash the radishes, then slice thinly. • Wash the lettuce leaves, shake dry and line four bowls with them. • Drain the rollmops or herring fillets, and cut into bite-sized pieces. • Pour two-thirds of the herb dressing into four bowls. Arrange the herring, cucumber and radishes on top, then pour over the remaining dressing. • Garnish the salad with the lemon wedges and remaining herbs. • This dish goes very well with wholemeal bread and butter.

Carpaccio Salad with Chicken Breast

2 boneless, skinless chicken breasts
3cm/1½-inch piece fresh root ginger
½ tsp chopped fresh aniseed or dill
Salt and freshly ground white pepper
1 celery heart
1 apple
1 small red pepper
4 slices canned pineapple in juice
2 tbsps olive oil
150ml/5fl oz crème fraîche
Juice of 1 lemon
4 kiwi fruit
4 radicchio leaves

Preparation time:
45 minutes
Nutritional value:
Analysis per serving, approx:
- 1800kJ/430kcal
- 27g protein
- 22g fat
- 32g carbohydrate

Rinse the chicken breasts in cold water and pat dry. • Peel and grate the ginger. Mix together half the ginger, the aniseed or dill and ½ tsp salt. • Rub this mixture into the chicken breasts and set aside. • Wash and dice the celery heart. Peel, core and dice the apple. Halve, seed, wash and dice the red pepper. Drain and dice the pineapple slices. Mix together the diced vegetables. • Heat the oil, and fry the chicken breasts for 3 minutes. Turn the chicken breasts, season with salt and pepper and fry for a further 3 minutes. • Mix together the crème fraîche, the remaining ginger and the lemon juice, and season to taste with salt and pepper. Pour the dressing over the diced vegetables. • Peel and slice the kiwi fruit. • Wash the radicchio leaves. • Arrange the radicchio leaves on a serving plate and spoon the diced vegetables on top. • Thinly slice the chicken breasts, and arrange them next to the salad. Garnish with the kiwi.

Carpaccio Salad with Monkfish

250g/8oz monkfish fillet
1 bunch of tarragon
2 tsps green peppercorns
150g/5½oz cherry tomatoes
1 small cucumber
2 shallots
150g/5½oz mushrooms
2 tbsps tarragon vinegar
1 tsp tarragon mustard
3 tbsps grapeseed oil
¼ tsp sugar
Salt and freshly ground white pepper
Some lettuce leaves

Preparation time:
15 minutes
Standing time:
1 hour
Arrangement time:
½ hour
Nutritional value:
Analysis per serving, approx:
- 500kJ/120kcal
- 12g protein
- 5g fat
- 7g carbohydrate

Rinse the fish under cold running water and pat dry. • Wash the tarragon, shake dry and chop finely. Crush the green peppercorns in a mortar with a pestle. • Rub the tarragon and peppercorns into the fish, wrap it in foil and place in the freezer for 1 hour. • Skin the tomatoes. • Peel and halve the cucumber, and scoop out the seeds. Scoop out balls of cucumber with a melon baller. • Peel and finely chop the shallots. Trim, wash and slice the mushrooms. • Beat together the vinegar, mustard, oil and sugar, and season to taste with salt and pepper. Lightly toss the tomatoes, cucumber, shallots and mushrooms in the dressing. • Wash and dry the lettuce leaves, and arrange them on a salad platter. • Slice the fish very thinly, and arrange it on one side of the platter. Season lightly with salt. Spoon the mixed salad onto the lettuce leaves.

Beef and Beetroot Salad

400g/14oz cold lean cooked beef
150g/5½oz pickled beetroot
1 large pickled gherkin
2 onions
100g/4oz canned sweetcorn
3 tbsps red wine vinegar
1 tsp English mustard
2 tbsps finely chopped fresh herbs (such as marjoram, parsley, chives, basil)
4 tbsps sunflower oil
Salt and freshly ground black pepper

Preparation time:
30 minutes
Standing time:
2 hours
Nutritional value:
Analysis per serving, approx:
- 1210kJ/290kcal
- 24g protein
- 15g fat
- 15g carbohydrate

Cut the beef into matchstick strips. • Dice the beetroot and reserve 1 tbsp of juice. Dice the gherkin. • Peel and thinly slice the onions, and push out into rings. Drain the sweetcorn. • Beat together the vinegar, reserved beetroot juice, mustard, herbs and oil, and season to taste with salt and pepper. • Place the beef, beetroot, gherkin, onion and sweetcorn in a salad bowl. Pour over the dressing and leave to stand for at least 2 hours.

Green Bean and Beef Salad

500g/1lb 2oz green beans
1 l/1³/₄ pints water
Salt and freshly ground black pepper
400g/14oz cold cooked lean beef
1 large onion
2 tomatoes
2 hard-boiled eggs, shelled
4 tbsps mayonnaise
2 tbsps tomato ketchup
200ml/7fl oz soured cream
1 tbsp red wine vinegar
Pinch of sugar
1 small round lettuce
2 tbsps finely chopped fresh parsley

Preparation time:
45 minutes
Nutritional value:
Analysis per serving, approx:
- 1890kJ/450kcal
- 34g protein
- 27g fat
- 20g carbohydrate

Wash, top and tail and chop the beans. Bring the water to the boil, add ¹/₂ tsp of salt and the beans and cook for 20 minutes. • Cut the beef into matchstick strips. Peel and finely dice the onion. • Wash and dry the tomatoes, and cut into eight. • Cut the eggs into quarters. • Mix together the mayonnaise, tomato ketchup, soured cream, vinegar and sugar, and season to taste with salt and pepper. • Separate the lettuce leaves, wash and shake dry. Line a salad bowl with the lettuce. • Drain the beans and allow to cool slightly. Gently mix together the beans, beef, onion and tomatoes. Pour over the dressing, toss well and spoon the salad onto the lettuce leaves. • Garnish with the eggs, and sprinkle over the parsley.

Our Tip: *Leftovers from the Sunday joint are ideally suited to this recipe.*

Pepper and Tomato Salad with Beef

500g/1lb 2oz green peppers
500g/1lb 2oz tomatoes
1 bunch of spring onions
200g/7oz cold roast beef, thinly sliced
2 hard-boiled eggs, shelled
3 tbsps red wine vinegar
1 tsp English mustard
½ tsp paprika
3 tbsps olive oil
Salt and freshly ground black pepper
2 tbsps finely chopped fresh parsley

Preparation time:
30 minutes
Nutritional value:
Analysis per serving, approx:
- 1210kJ/290kcal
- 21g protein
- 16g fat
- 14g carbohydrate

Halve, seed, wash and dry the peppers. Cut into strips. • Wash, dry and slice the tomatoes. • Trim, wash and finely chop the spring onions. • Cut the beef into strips. • Slice the eggs. • Place the peppers, tomatoes, spring onions, beef and eggs in a salad bowl, and mix gently. • Beat together the vinegar, mustard, paprika and oil, and season to taste with salt and pepper. Pour the dressing over the salad. Sprinkle with parsley. • Cover and leave to stand until you are ready to serve. • Buttered crusty rye rolls make a tasty accompaniment.

Our Tip: Yellow peppers also taste delicious in this salad.

New Year's Eve Salad

To serve 8:
8 smoked mackerel fillets
1 head of celery
400g/14oz cold cooked beef
500g/1lb 2oz boiled potatoes
250g/8oz pickled beetroot
2 pickled gherkins
2 onions
1 large tart apple
225ml/8fl oz mayonnaise
300ml/10fl oz soured cream
1 tsp vinegar
1 tsp creamed horseradish or horseradish sauce
3 hard-boiled eggs, shelled
Salt and freshly ground white pepper
Lettuce leaves
3 tbsps finely chopped fresh parsley

Soaking time:
1 hour
Preparation time:
1 hour
Standing time:
3-4 hours

Nutritional value:
Analysis per serving, approx:
- 3500kJ/830kcal
- 45g protein
- 62g fat
- 27g carbohydrate

Cut the fish into bite-sized pieces. • Trim, wash and finely chop the celery. Dice the beef. Peel and dice the potatoes. Drain and dice the beetroot and gherkins. Peel and finely chop the onions. Peel, quarter, core and dice the apple. • Beat together the mayonnaise, soured cream, vinegar and creamed horseradish or horseradish sauce, and season to taste with salt and pepper. • Mix together the fish, celery, beef, potatoes, beetroot, gherkins, onions and apple in a bowl. Pour over the dressing, and leave to stand for 3-4 hours. • Cut the eggs into eight. Divide the lettuce leaves between eight individual plates, and top with the salad. Garnish with the eggs and parsley.

Belgian Egg Salad

To serve 8:
200ml/7fl oz mayonnaise
2 tsps tomato purée
3 tbsps lemon juice
6-8 tbsps water
1 small onion
$^1/_2$ tsp sugar
Salt and freshly ground black pepper
8 potatoes, cooked in their skins
2 gherkins
2 apples
4 heads of chicory
1 bunch of radishes
10 hard-boiled eggs, shelled

Preparation time:
50 minutes
Standing time:
1 hour
Nutritional value:
Analysis per serving, approx:
- 1890kJ/450kcal
- 20g protein
- 28g fat
- 32g carbohydrate

Beat together the mayonnaise, tomato purée, lemon juice and water. Peel and grate the onion, and stir it into the dressing. Stir in the sugar, and season to taste with salt and pepper. • Peel and dice the potatoes. Finely dice the gherkins. Peel, quarter, core and thinly slice the apples. • Place the potatoes, gherkins and apples in a salad bowl, and pour over the dressing. Mix gently, and leave to stand for 1 hour. • Trim the chicory and cut out the bitter centres of the stems. Separate the leaves, wash, shake dry and cut into strips. • Trim, wash and slice the radishes. • Cut the eggs into eight. • Gently mix the chicory and radishes into the salad. Garnish with the eggs.

Oakleaf Lettuce with Chicken Livers

1 head of oakleaf lettucee
400g/14oz chicken livers
2 tbsps vegetable cooking fat
Salt and freshly ground white pepper
1 small garlic clove
1 tbsp cider vinegar
2 tbsps sunflower oil
2 tbsps finely chopped fresh parsley

Preparation time:
40 minutes
Nutritional value:
Analysis per serving, approx:
- 970kJ/230kcal
- 23g protein
- 14g fat
- 4g carbohydrate

Separate the oakleaf lettuce into leaves, wash and shake dry. • Wash the chicken livers and pat dry. Remove any fat and score each liver at its thickest point. • Heat the cooking fat, and fry the chicken livers over a high heat, turning frequently, for about 3 minutes until browned on all sides. Remove from the heat, and season to taste with salt and pepper. • Crush the garlic. Beat together the vinegar and sunflower oil. Stir in the garlic, and season to taste with salt and pepper. • Tear the oakleaf lettuce leaves into 4cm/2-inch pieces and toss lightly in the dressing. Arrange the leaves on a serving plate and top with the chicken livers. • Sprinkle over the parsley just before serving.

Our Tip: You may use endive, iceberg lettuce or lamb's lettuce as a substitute for the oakleaf lettuce.

Rice Salad with Yogurt Dressing

250ml/9fl oz chicken stock
300g/10oz boneless chicken breast
500ml/17fl oz water
Salt and freshly ground white pepper
100g/4oz long-grain rice
2 tbsps raisins
4 mandarins
150ml/5fl oz natural yogurt
2 tbsps mayonnaise
3 tbsps lemon juice
2 tbsps soya sauce
1 tsp curry powder
2 bananas

Preparation time:
30 minutes
Standing time:
30 minutes
Nutritional value:
Analysis per serving, approx:
- 1380kJ/330kcal
- 22g protein
- 5g fat
- 54g carbohydrate

Heat the chicken stock in a pan. • Add the chicken breast, cover and cook over a gentle heat for 20 minutes. • Bring the water to boil and add $1/2$ tsp salt. Add the rice, stir once and simmer, uncovered, over a moderate heat for 10 minutes. Add the raisins, and cook for a further 5 minutes, or until the rice is tender. Drain, rinse in cold water and drain again. • Peel 2 of the mandarins and separate into segments. Squeeze the juice of the remaining mandarins. • Pour the mandarin juice into a salad bowl, and stir in the yogurt, mayonnaise, lemon juice, soya sauce and curry powder, and season to taste with pepper. • Skin and dice the chicken. • Stir 6 tbsps of the chicken stock into the yogurt dressing. • Place the chicken, rice mixture and mandarin segments in the salad bowl. Peel and slice the bananas, add them to the bowl and mix thoroughly. • Leave to stand for 30 minutes.

Spanish Rice Salad

To serve 6:
500ml/17fl oz water
Salt and freshly ground black pepper
200g/7oz long-grain rice
2 green peppers
500g/1lb 2oz tomatoes
½ cold cooked chicken
200g/7oz cooked peeled prawns
180g/6oz can tuna fish
2 onions
100g/4oz stoned black olives
6 tbsps red wine vinegar
4 tbsps extra-virgin olive oil
½ tsp sweet paprika
4 canned anchovy fillets, drained
2 tbsps finely chopped fresh parsley

Preparation time:
45 minutes
Nutritional value:
Analysis per serving, approx:
- 2980kJ/710kcal
- 55g protein
- 32g fat
- 55g carbohydrate

Bring the water to the boil, add ½ tsp salt and the rice. Simmer over a gentle heat for 15 minutes. • Halve, seed and wash the peppers, and cut into strips. • Wash the tomatoes and cut them into eight. • Remove the chicken meat from the bones and dice. • Rinse and drain the prawns. Drain and flake the tuna fish. • Peel and finely chop the onions. • Drain the rice and leave to cool slightly. • Mix together the peppers, tomatoes, chicken, prawns, tuna, onions and olives in a salad bowl. Gently stir in the rice. • Beat together the vinegar, oil and paprika, and season to taste with salt and pepper. Pound the anchovy fillets with a pestle in a mortar, and add to the dressing. Pour the dressing over the salad and garnish with the parsley.

Tofu and Mango Salad

400g/14oz tofu
2 tbsps sesame seeds
1 small head oakleaf lettuce
1 large, ripe mango
2 tbsps soya sauce
Freshly ground black pepper
3 tbsps sesame oil
2 tbsps lemon juice
125ml/4fl oz double cream
1-2 tsps finely grated fresh root ginger
2 tsps clear honey
1 tbsp snipped chives

Preparation time:
40 minutes
Nutritional value:
Analysis per serving, approx:
- 1510kJ/360kcal
- 11g protein
- 25g fat
- 25g carbohydrate

Cut the tofu into 1cm/$^1/_2$-inch slices. Lay them on a clean, folded tea towel, cover with a board, weigh it down and leave for about 15 minutes. • Meanwhile, toast the sesame seeds in a pan over a moderate heat, turning frequently. • Separate the oakleaf lettuce into leaves, wash and shake dry. • Peel the mango and cut the flesh into thin strips and discard the stone. • Drizzle half the soya sauce over the tofu slices and sprinkle with pepper. • Heat 1 tbsp of the sesame oil in a pan, and fry the tofu slices, seasoned side down, for about 5 minutes. Pour over the remaining soy sauce and season with pepper again. Turn the tofu, and fry for a further 5 minutes. • Beat together 1 tbsp of the remaining oil and half the lemon juice. Toss the salad leaves in this mixture, and arrange in a salad bowl. • Mix together the cream, the remaining oil and lemon juice, the ginger, honey and chives to make a dressing, and pour over the salad. Arrange the mango slices on top and scatter over half the sesame seeds. Dice the tofu, arrange it in the bowl, and sprinkle over the remaining sesame seeds.

Oakleaf Lettuce Salad
with Cheesy Croûtons

1 head oakleaf lettuce
2 thick slices day-old white bread
2 garlic cloves
5 tbsps extra-virgin olive oil
2 tbsps grated fresh Pecorino or Parmesan cheese
2 tbsps herb vinegar
Salt and freshly ground black pepper

Preparation time:
20 minutes
Nutritional value:
Analysis per serving, approx:
• 630kJ/150kcal
• 7g protein
• 7g fat
• 14g carbohydrate

Trim the lettuce, chop the leaves into broad strips, rinse under cold water and drain. • Dice the bread. • Crush the garlic, and stir into the olive oil. • Heat 1 tbsp of the flavoured oil in a small pan and fry the bread cubes until golden brown. Sprinkle over the grated cheese and continue to fry, turning frequently, until the cheese melts. • Season the vinegar with salt and pepper to taste, and beat in the remaining olive oil. Put the lettuce in a serving bowl, and pour over the dressing. • Garnish with the cheese croûtons before serving.

Our Tip: *You can use any sort of lettuce for this recipe – experiment with lamb's lettuce, frisée, endive or even an ordinary round lettuce. Growing your own lettuce is ideal, as this guarantees fresh produce in spring, summer and autumn.*

Buckwheat Salad

1l/1¾ pints water
Salt and freshly ground black pepper
½ tsp dried thyme
1 small bay leaf
2 tbsps sunflower oil
100g/4oz buckwheat
3 tomatoes
3 shallots
25g/1oz canned anchovy fillets, drained
150ml/5fl oz soured cream
1 tbsp lemon juice
2 tbsps snipped fresh chives

Preparation time:
40 minutes
Nutritional value:
Analysis per serving, approx:
- 1210kJ/290kcal
- 7g protein
- 17g fat
- 27g carbohydrate

Bring the water to the boil with ½ tsp salt, the thyme, bay leaf and 1 tbsp of the oil. Add the buckwheat grains and cook, uncovered, for 15 minutes. Remove the pan from the heat and leave to stand for 5 minutes. Drain and leave to cool. Remove and discard the bay leaf. • Skin and thinly slice the tomatoes. • Peel and thinly slice 2 of the shallots and push out into rings. Peel and finely chop the remaining shallot. • Chop one-third of the anchovy fillets very finely and cut the remaining fillets in half lengthways. • Mix together the soured cream, the remaining oil, the lemon juice, pepper to taste, chopped shallots, chopped anchovies and half the chives. Stir about two-thirds of the dressing into the buckwheat grains. • Arrange the tomato slices and onion rings around the edge of a serving plate, and spoon the buckwheat salad into the centre. Arrange the sliced anchovy fillets on top, pour over the remaining dressing and garnish with the remaining chives.

Caponata

500g/1lb 2oz aubergines
Salt and freshly ground black pepper
250g/8oz onions
250g/8oz tomatoes
1 small head of celery
75g/3oz stoned green olives
6 tbsps olive oil
1 tbsp capers
2 tbsps sultanas
1 tbsp pine nuts
125ml/5 fl oz white wine vinegar
1 tbsp sugar

Preparation time:
1½ hours
Cooling time:
2 hours
Nutritional value:
Analysis per serving, approx:
- 880kJ/210kcal
- 5g protein
- 11g fat
- 23g carbohydrate

Wash and dice the aubergines. Place in a colander, sprinkle over 1 tsp salt and set aside for 30 minutes to drain. • Peel and thinly slice the onions and push out into rings. • Skin the tomatoes, and chop finely. • Separate and wash the celery. Chop into 3cm/1-inch pieces. Blanch in a little boiling water for 5 minutes, and drain. • Coarsely chop the olives. • Rinse the aubergines and pat dry. • Heat 4 tbsps of the oil in a pan, and fry the aubergines over a high heat for a few minutes. Remove and drain on absorbent paper. Add the remaining oil to the pan and reduce the heat. Fry the onion rings until translucent. Add the celery and fry for 2 minutes. Add the tomatoes, and cook for 5 minutes. Stir in the olives, capers, sultanas, pine nuts and aubergines. • Season to taste with salt and pepper, add the vinegar and sugar, and simmer for a further 10 minutes until the vinegar has evaporated. Leave to cool completely before serving.

Potato and Bean Salad

To serve 8:
2 kg/4½lbs waxy potatoes
500g/1lb 2oz green beans
2 sprigs savory
Salt and freshly ground white pepper
1 garlic clove
2 onions
2 tbsps finely chopped fresh thyme
125ml/4fl oz hot chicken stock
125ml/4fl oz wine vinegar
2 tsps Dijon mustard
¼ tsp sugar
8 tomatoes
400g/14oz Feta cheese
100g/4oz pimiento-stuffed green olives
50g/2oz stoned black olives
2 tbsps finely chopped fresh parsley
1 tbsp torn fresh basil leaves
4 tbsps sunflower oil
4 tbsps olive oil

Preparation time:
1 hour
Standing time:
1 hour
Nutritional value:
Analysis per serving, approx:
- 1680kJ/400kcal
- 14g protein
- 16g fat
- 53g carbohydrate

Wash the potatoes. Place in a pan, cover with water, bring to the boil and simmer for 20 minutes. • Trim, wash and chop the beans. Place the beans in a pan, add 200ml/7fl oz water, the savory and a pinch of salt, cover, bring to the boil and cook for 15 minutes. Drain. • Drain and peel the potatoes, and cut into quarters. • Cut the garlic clove in half and rub the cut sides around the inside of a salad bowl. Put the potatoes and beans in the bowl. Peel and finely chop the onions. Add the onions and thyme to the salad, and season to taste with salt and pepper. • Mix together the stock, vinegar, mustard and sugar, pour it over the salad and stir thoroughly. • Cover and leave to stand for 1 hour. • Cut the

tomatoes into eight, and dice the cheese. • Add the tomatoes, cheese, green and black olives, parsley and basil to the salad, pour over the sunflower oil and olive oil and mix thoroughly.

Wholewheat Pasta Salad

To serve 8:
2 l/3½ pints water
1 tbsp cardamom seeds
Salt and freshly ground white pepper
300g/10oz wholewheat pasta spirals
75g/3oz unhulled sesame seeds
200ml/7fl oz cream
4 tbsps lemon juice
2 tbsps sesame oil
2 tbsps soya sauce
2-3 tsps curry powder
½ tsp ground turmeric
1.5 kg/3½lbs pineapple
6 bananas
3 tbsps snipped chives

Preparation time:
40 minutes
Standing time:
10 minutes
Nutritional value:
Analysis per serving, approx:
- 2020kJ/480kcal
- 10g protein
- 18g fat
- 65g carbohydrate

Bring water to the boil in a large pan. Add the cardamom seeds, 1 tsp salt and pasta and cook for 10-12 minutes or until tender but still firm to the bite. Drain, rinse briefly under cold water and leave to cool. • Fry the sesame seeds in a dry heavy pan until they start to pop and release their fragrance. Remove from the heat and set aside. • Beat together cream, lemon juice, oil, soya sauce, curry powder and turmeric, and season to taste with pepper. • Peel, core and dice the pineapple. • Peel and thickly slice the bananas. • Combine the pasta, pineapple, bananas, sesame seeds and chives in a salad bowl. Pour over dressing and mix gently. Leave the salad to stand for no longer than 10 minutes. Adjust the seasoning by adding a little more curry powder or pepper if you like a spicy salad.

Spaghetti and Salami Salad

To serve 8:
250g/8oz borlotti beans
1 l/1³/₄ pints water
1 bay leaf
1 bouquet garni
250g/8oz spaghetti
2 l/3¹/₂ pints boiling water
Salt and freshly ground black pepper
250g/8oz red skin onions
250g/8oz salami, thinly sliced
125ml/4fl oz red wine vinegar
2 tsps sweet paprika
125ml/4fl oz olive oil
2 tbsps finely chopped fresh parsley

Soaking time:
12 hours
Preparation time:
40 minutes
Standing time:
10 minutes
Nutritional value:
Analysis per serving, approx:
- 1390kJ/330kcal
- 12g protein
- 21g fat
- 27g carbohydrate

Soak the borlotti beans overnight in the cold water. • Transfer the beans and the soaking water to a large pan. Add the bay leaf and bouquet garni, bring to the boil and simmer for about 30 minutes until tender. Drain and discard the bay leaf and bouquet garni. • Cook the spaghetti in the boiling water for 15 minutes. Drain, rinse briefly under cold water and drain again. • Peel the onions, cut in half lengthways, then thinly slice crossways. Cut the salami into thin strips. • Place the beans, spaghetti, onions and salami in a salad bowl. Beat together the vinegar, paprika and oil, and season to taste with salt and pepper. Pour the dressing over the salad. • Leave to stand for 10 minutes, then stir in the parsley.

Kale and Soya Bean Salad

100g/4oz yellow soya beans
1 tsp vegetable stock granules
1 bay leaf
500g/1lb 2oz kale
150g/5¹/₂oz bean sprouts
1 red skin onion
3 tbsps safflower oil
3 tbsps red wine vinegar
2 tbsps soya sauce
Freshly ground black pepper

Soaking time:
12 hours
Preparation time:
2 hours
Standing time:
10 minutes
Nutritional value:
Analysis per serving, approx:
- 1000kJ/240kcal
- 18g protein
- 10g fat
- 18g carbohydrate

Soak the soya beans overnight in 500ml/17fl oz of cold water. • Drain and place in a pan with 500ml/17fl oz fresh water, the stock granules and bay leaf. Bring to the boil and cook for 1¹/₂-2 hours until soft but not mushy. Drain and discard the bay leaf. • Meanwhile, wash the kale and discard any tough stalks. Blanch the leaves in boiling water for 10 minutes. Drain, allow to cool slightly, and chop coarsely. • Wash the bean sprouts, blanch in boiling water for 5 minutes and drain. • Peel and halve the onion, and slice thinly crossways. • Place the beans in a bowl while they are still warm. Add the kale, bean sprouts, oil, vinegar, soya sauce and onion, and mix well. Season generously with pepper. • Leave to stand for about 10 minutes. • This salad is best served when still slightly warm, and is delicious with crispy fried potatoes.

Chinese Leaves with Grapes

50g/2oz sesame seeds
125g/5oz green grapes
125g/5oz black grapes
250g/8oz Chinese leaves
100g/4oz lamb's lettuce
2 tbsps lemon juice
2 tsps clear honey
¼ tsp ground ginger
Pinch of ground cloves
2 tbsps sesame oil
Freshly ground white pepper

Preparation time:
30 minutes
Nutritional value:
Analysis per serving, approx:
- 760kJ/180kcal
- 4g protein
- 11g fat
- 17g carbohydrate

Fry the sesame seeds in a heavy, dry pan, stirring constantly, until they begin to brown and give off an aroma. Remove from the heat and set aside. • Wash, halve and seed the grapes. • Trim the Chinese leaves and discard any blemished leaves. Wash, drain well and cut crossways into strips. • Wash the lamb's lettuce, remove any damaged leaves and drain well. • Mix together the lemon juice, honey, ginger and cloves, and beat in the sesame oil. Season with pepper to taste. Place the grapes, Chinese leaves and lamb's lettuce in a salad bowl, pour over the dressing and toss lightly. Scatter the sesame seeds on top to garnish.

Our Tip: Why not ring the changes and replace the sesame seeds and sesame oil with coarsely chopped walnuts and walnut oil, or toasted sunflower seeds and sunflower oil?

Italian Salad

1 kg/2¼lbs green asparagus
Salt and freshly ground white pepper
1 sugar cube
250g/8oz button mushrooms
15g/½oz butter
2-3 firm tomatoes
3 tbsps wine vinegar
Pinch of paprika
5 tbsps olive oil
2 tbsps finely chopped fresh parsley

Preparation time:
45 minutes
Standing time:
30 minutes
Nutritional value:
Analysis per serving, approx:
• 630kJ/150kcal
• 8g protein
• 7g fat
• 15g carbohydrate

Wash the asparagus and cut off the woody ends. Tie loosely together in bundles of six spears. Fill a tall saucepan with enough water just to cover the asparagus, preferably standing up. Add 1 tsp salt and the sugar cube, and bring to the boil. Cover and simmer for 15-20 minutes. • Trim, wash and slice the mushrooms. Melt the butter, and gently fry the mushrooms for 10 minutes. Remove from the heat, sprinkle with a little salt and leave to cool. • Skin and seed the tomatoes. Dice the flesh. • Drain the asparagus, and cut into 4cm/2-inch long pieces. Combine the asparagus, mushrooms and tomatoes in a salad bowl. • Mix together the vinegar and paprika, and beat in the oil. Season to taste with salt and pepper. Pour the dressing over the salad and toss lightly. • Leave to stand for 30 minutes before serving, garnished with the parsley.

Mixed Salad Platter

1 celeriac
250g/8oz cauliflower
4 small tomatoes
300g/10oz cucumber
4 small carrots
1 red pepper
1 onion
100g/4oz lamb's lettuce
100g/4oz radicchio
12 stuffed olives
½ tsp coarsely ground black pepper
4 tbsps olive oil
3 tbsps wine vinegar
½ tsp salt
1 tbsp freshly chopped mixed herbs
1 pot natural yogurt (150g/5½oz)
1 hard-boiled egg

Preparation time:
20 minutes
Cooking time:
20 minutes
Nutritional value:
Analysis per serving, approx:
- 1115kJ/265kcal
- 9g protein
- 15g fat
- 24g carbohydrate

Wash the celeriac and cook for 20 minutes in water to cover in a saucepan with the lid on. Drain. • Break the cauliflower into florets and boil in salted water for 10 minutes. • Wash, dry and quarter the tomatoes. Wash and slice the cucumber thinly. Scrape, wash and grate the carrots. Halve the pepper, remove the pith and seeds, and cut into strips. Peel the onion and cut into rings. Clean, wash and drain the lamb's lettuce and radicchio. Tear the radicchio into large pieces. Halve the olives. Peel the cooked celeriac and slice with a stainless steel knife. Drain the cauliflower florets. • Arrange all the salad ingredients in sections on a large serving plate, and sprinkle with pepper. Arrange the olives on top. • Combine the oil, vinegar, salt, herbs and yogurt

and pour this sauce over the salad. • Shell the egg, cut it into eight wedges, and use to garnish the salad.

Wild Herb Salad with Croûtons

200g/7oz mixed wild herbs, e.g. young dandelion leaves, sorrel, dead nettle leaves, ribwort, plantain leaves
1 lettuce (150g/5½oz)
1 small apple
1 tsp maple syrup
1 tsp lemon juice
3 tbsps walnut oil
1 tbsp apple vinegar
1 tbsp apple juice
¼ tsp salt
2 tbsps chopped chives
2 slices wholewheat bread
1 clove garlic
2 tbsps vegetable margarine

Preparation time:
30 minutes
Nutritional value:
Analysis per serving, approx:
- 670kJ/160kcal
- 3g protein
- 8g fat
- 19g carbohydrate

Wash the wild herbs thoroughly, removing any long stems, and drain. Break the lettuce into leaves, wash well, and drain. Tear larger leaves into several pieces. Roughly chop the drained herbs, and mix them with the lettuce in a bowl. • Quarter, peel and core the apple, then cut into thin sticks. Mix these with the syrup, lemon juice, oil, vinegar, apple juice and salt. Toss the salad and the chives in this sauce. • Cut the bread into 1cm/½-inch cubes. Peel and crush the garlic. Mix the crushed garlic into the margarine, melt in a frying-pan, and fry the cubes of bread until golden. • Scatter these croûtons over the salad.

Spinach Salad with Orange

400g/14oz very young spinach leaves
2 untreated oranges
1 apple
1 tbsp walnut oil
¼ tsp salt
½ tsp ginger syrup
1 pot natural yogurt (150g/5½oz)
4 tbsps coarsely grated Jerusalem artichoke

Preparation time:
20 minutes
Nutritional value:
Analysis per serving, approx:
- 545kJ/130kcal
- 5g protein
- 4g fat
- 19g carbohydrate

Pick over the spinach leaves, wash and shake dry; remove the long stems and cut larger leaves in half. Peel 1 orange, and cut it into segments, removing any pips. Remove a thin layer of peel from the second orange, and cut into julienne strips. Squeeze out the juice. Peel, core and quarter the apple, and thinly slice the quarters. Put the spinach, orange and apple in a salad bowl. • Mix the orange juice, oil, salt, ginger syrup and yogurt together, and toss the salad ingredients in this sauce. Scatter the Jerusalem artichoke and strips of orange peel over the salad.

Our Tip: *If Jerusalem artichoke is not available, cut two pieces of stem ginger into tiny pieces and scatter them over the salad. If you do not like orange peel, substitute coarsely chopped walnuts.*

Index

Artichoke Cocktail 10
Beef and Beetroot Salad 36
Belgian Egg Salad 41
Breast of Goose with Peppers 8
Buckwheat Salad 49
Caponata 50
Carpaccio Salad with Chicken Breast 34
Carpaccio Salad with Monkfish 35
Celery and Endive Salad 23
Chinese Leaf and Orange Salad 12
Chinese Leaves with Grapes 58
Coconut Fruit Platter 13
Courgette Salad with Black Olives 22
Cucumber and Prawn Salad 14
Cucumber Cocktail 16
Fennel and Turkey Salad 17
Four Seasons Salad 27
Fruit on Iceberg Lettuce Salad 11
Golden Salad 28
Greek Salad 19
Green Bean and Beef Salad 37
Herring and Cucumber Salad 32
Italian Salad 59
Kale and Soya Bean Salad 56
Lamb's Lettuce Salad with Pork Fillet 9
Lamb's Lettuce with Radicchio 30
Mixed Salad Platter 60
Mixed Salad 29
Mussel Cocktail 7
New Year's Eve Salad 40
Oakleaf Lettuce Salad with Cheesy Croûtons 48
Oakleaf Lettuce with Chicken Livers 42
Oakleaf Lettuce with Smoked Salmon 15
Pepper and Salami Salad 20
Pepper and Tomato Salad with Beef 38
Potato and Bean Salad 52
Radicchio and Cheese Salad 21
Radicchio with Roquefort Dressing 31
Rice Salad with Yogurt Dressing 44
Sicilian Shallots 24
Spaghetti and Salami Salad 55
Spanish Rice Salad 45
Spinach Salad with Orange 63
Tofu and Mango Salad 46
Tomato Salad 26
Tuna Fish Salad 18
Wholewheat Pasta Salad 54
Wild Herb Salad with Croûtons 62